Happy

A happy mixture of old favourites and modern poems, this collection has been specially chosen to appeal to very young children.

But to listen to or to read, this is a delightful new anthology which opens all children's minds to the strange new world of poetry.

Cover design by Desmond Clover

Happy Landings

Poems for the Youngest
chosen and arranged by
Howard Sergeant

Illustrations by Desmond Clover

Evans Brothers Limited London

Published by Evans Brothers Limited
Montague House, Russell Square, London, W.C.1

First published 1971
Fourth printing 1974

For Cherrill and Oriel

Set in 12 on 15 pt. Imprint
and printed in Great Britain by
Cox & Wyman Ltd,
London, Reading and Fakenham
CSD ISBN 0 237 35189 7
PB ISBN 0 237 35190 0

PRA 4027

Contents

Acknowledgements

For permission to use copyright material the editor and publishers are indebted to the following:

The author for 'Finders-keepers' by Cicely Barnes; William Blackwood & Sons Ltd. for 'Daddy Fell into the Pond' by Alfred Noyes; Brontpress Ltd. for 'The Piffle-poffle' by Catherine Lodge; Dennis Dobson Ltd. for 'Look at all those Monkeys' from *Silly Verse for Kids* by Spike Milligan; the author for 'Four Little Girls', 'Grandma Gurney' and 'Three Warm Pennies' by A. E. Dudley; the author for 'Cat in Moonlight' by Douglas Gibson; the Hamlyn Publishing Group for 'Hurry Home' from *Here and There* by Leonard Clark; William Heinemann Ltd. for 'Rabbit and Lark' from *The Wandering Moon* by James Reeves; the author for 'Autumn Song' by Ted Hughes; the author for 'The May Tree' and 'Snow Maidens' by Norah Hussey; the author for 'I Had a Little Spaceman' by Michael Ivens; Macmillan & Co. Ltd. for 'I Took my Wife to Market', 'My Mother saw a Dancing Bear' and 'I Saw a Jolly Hunter' from *Figgie Hobbin* by Charles Causley and 'Skate' by Alan Brownjohn; Oxford University Press for 'Explorers' and 'Fireworks' from *The Blackbird in the Lilac* by James Reeves, and 'Cats' from *The Children's Bells* by Eleanor Farjeon; the author for 'Jumping Jane' and 'The Voyage' by Joan Prince; the author for 'Soft Landings' by Howard Sergeant; Wills & Hepworth Ltd. for 'Mr. Giraffe' from the *Ladybird Book of Bedtime Rhymes* by Geoffrey Lapage.

Introduction

When the astronaut soars into the sky in his space-ship for the first time, he looks back at the earth on which we live and sees everything in an exciting new way. Reading poetry is just like that; for the best poems open to us a strange new world; and yet it is still the world we have always known, with everything in its proper place. It is only our way of *looking at things* that has changed.

Some children for whom this book is intended will not, of course, be quite old enough to read it for themselves yet, but I know that they will have the same thrill as older children when it is read aloud to them by their parents, teachers, or older members of the family. To all who take this trip into the exciting new world of poetry – to young and not-so-young alike – I say: Enjoy your flight and happy landings!

Howard Sergeant

White Sheep

White sheep, white sheep
On a blue hill,
When the wind stops
You all stand still.

You all run away
When the winds blow;
White sheep, white sheep,
Where do you go?

W. H. Davies

The Rain

The rain is raining all around,
It falls on field and tree;
It rains on the umbrellas here
And on the ships at sea.

Robert Louis Stevenson

Little Johnny

Little Johnny fished all day,
Fishes would not come his way.
'Had enough of this,' said he,
'I'll be going home to tea!'

When the fishes saw him go,
Up they came all in a row;
Jumped about and laughed with glee,
Shouting, 'Johnny's gone to tea!'

One Misty, Moisty Morning

One misty, moisty morning,
When cloudy was the weather,
There I met an old man
Clothed all in leather;
Clothed all in leather,
With cap under his chin, –
How do you do, and how do you do,
And how do you do again?

The Cuckoo

Cuckoo, Cuckoo,
What do you do?

In April
I open my bill.

In May
I sing night and day.

In June
I change my tune.

In July
Away I fly.

In August
Go I must.

The Leaves are Green

The leaves are green,
The nuts are brown,
They hang so high
They will not come down.

Leave them alone
Till frosty weather,
Then they will all
Come down together.

The May Tree

When Maytime's in
the meadowside,
the Hawthorn tree
becomes a bride!

From top to toe
in perfect dress
she dazzles me
with loveliness –

White gloves, white veil
all country-sweet,
with white confetti
at her feet.

Norah Hussey

A White Hen Sitting

A white hen sitting
  On white eggs three:
Next, three speckled chickens
  As plump as plump can be.

An owl and a hawk
  And a bat came to see;
But chicks beneath their mother's wing
  Squat safe as safe can be.

Christina Rossetti

The Cow

The friendly cow all red and white,
  I love with all my heart:
She gives me cream with all her might,
  To eat with apple-tart.

She wanders lowing here and there,
  And yet she cannot stray,
All in the pleasant open air,
  The pleasant light of day.

And blown by all the winds that pass
  And wet with all the showers,
She walks among the meadow grass
  And eats the meadow flowers.

Robert Louis Stevenson

Birds on a Stone

There were two birds
  Sat on a stone.
One flew away,
  Then there was one.
The other flew after,
  Then there was none,
And so the poor stone
Was left all alone.

At the Seaside

When I was down beside the sea,
A wooden spade they gave to me
   To dig the sandy shore.

My holes were empty like a cup,
In every hole the sea came up,
   Till it could come no more.

Robert Louis Stevenson

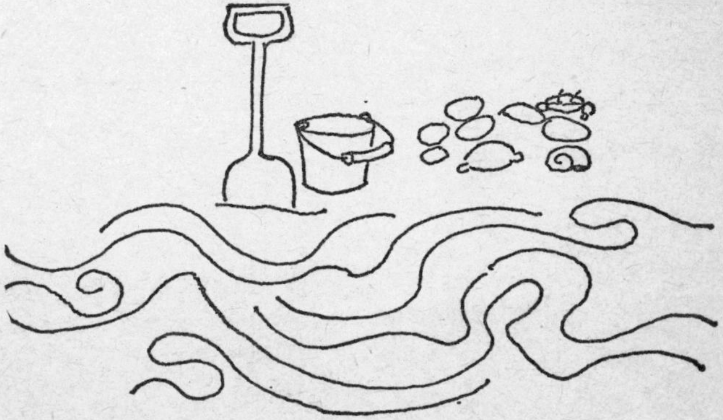

The Swing

How do you like to go up in a swing,
  Up in the air so blue?
Oh, I do think it the pleasantest thing
  Ever a child can do!

Up in the air and over the wall,
  Till I can see so wide,
Rivers and trees and cattle and all
  Over the countryside –

Till I look down on the garden green,
  Down on the roof so brown –
Up in the air I go flying again,
  Up in the air and down!

Robert Louis Stevenson

Grasshopper Green

Grasshopper Green is a comical chap;
He lives on the best of fare.
Bright little trousers, jacket and cap,
These are his summer wear.

Out in the meadow he loves to go,
Playing away in the sun;
It's hopperty, skipperty, high and low,
Summer's the time for fun.

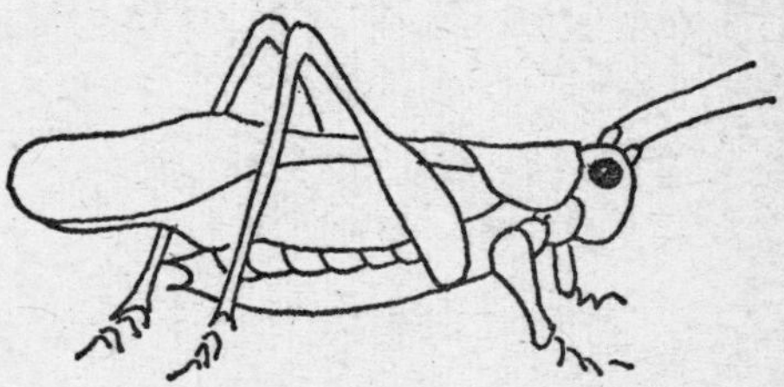

What the Leaves said

The leaves said, 'It's spring;
And here are we,
Opening and stretching
On every tree.'

The leaves said, 'It's summer;
Each bird has a nest;
We make the shadow
Where they can rest.'

The leaves said, 'It's autumn;
Aren't we all gay?'
Scarlet and golden
And russet were they.

The leaves said, 'It's winter;
Weary are we.'
So they lay down and slept
Under the tree.

Storm-wind

The wind has such a rainy sound
  Moaning through the town,
The sea has such a windy sound –
  Will the ships go down?

The apples in the orchard
  Tumble from their tree –
Oh will the ships go down, go down,
  In the windy sea?

Christina Rossetti

Robinson Crusoe

Poor old Robinson Crusoe!
Poor old Robinson Crusoe!
They made him a coat
Of an old nanny goat,
I wonder how they could do so!
With a ring a ting tang
And a ring a ting tang.
Poor old Robinson Crusoe!

The Gabelory Man

Follow my gabelory man,
Follow my gabelory man.
I'll do all that ever I can
To follow my gabelory man.

We'll borrow a horse and steal a gig,
And round the world we'll have a jig,
And I'll do all that ever I can
To follow my gabelory man.

Robert Barnes

Robert Barnes, fellow fine,
Can you shoe this horse of mine?

Yes, good sir, that I can,
As well as any other man:

There's a nail and there's a prod,
And now, good sir, your horse is shod.

Autumn Fires

In the other gardens
  And all up the vale,
From the autumn bonfires
  See the smoke trail!

Pleasant summer over
  And all the summer flowers,
The red fire blazes,
  The grey smoke towers.

Sing a song of seasons!
  Something bright in all!
Flowers in the summer,
  Fires in the fall.

Robert Louis Stevenson

The Little Rain

The great rain is over,
The little rain begun,
Falling from the higher leaves,
Bright in the sun,
Down to the lower leaves,
One drop by one.

Mary Coleridge

Autumn Song

There came a day that caught the summer
Wrung its neck
Plucked it
And ate it.

Now what shall I do with the trees?
The day said, the day said.
Strip them bare, strip them bare.
Let's see what is really there.

And what shall I do with the sun?
The day said, the day said.
Roll him away till he's cold and small.
He'll come back rested if he comes back at all.

And what shall I do with the birds?
The day said, the day said.
The birds I've frightened, let them flit,
I'll hang out pork for the brave tomtit.

And what shall I do with the seed?
The day said, the day said.
Bury it deep, see what it's worth.
See if it can stand the earth.

What shall I do with the people?
The day said, the day said.
Stuff them with apple and blackberry pie –
They'll love me then till the day they die.

There came this day and he was autumn.
His mouth was wide
And red as a sunset.
His tail was an icicle.

Ted Hughes

Oats and Beans and Barley

Oats and beans and barley grow!
Oats and beans and barley grow!
Do you or I or anyone know
How oats and beans and barley grow?

First the farmer sows his seed,
Then he stands and takes his ease,
Stamps his feet and *claps* his hands,
And *turns around* to view the land.
Waiting for a partner,
Waiting for a partner!
Open the ring and take one in.

Now you are married you must obey,
You must be true to all you say.
You must be wise, you must be good
And help your wife to chop the wood.

Children's game

Mr Giraffe

O Mister Giraffe, you make me laugh,
You seem to be made all wrong;
Your head is so high up there in the sky
And your neck is so very long
That your dinner and tea, it seems to me,
Have such a long way to go,
And I'm wondering how they manage to know
The way to your tummy below.

Geoffrey Lapage

Just Like Me

I went up one pair of stairs.
  Just like me

I went up two pairs of stairs.
  Just like me

I went into a room.
  Just like me

I looked out of the window.
  Just like me

And there I saw a monkey.
  Just like me

If I were an apple

If I were an apple
And grew upon a tree,
I think I'd fall down
On a nice boy like me.
I wouldn't stay there
Giving nobody joy;
I'd fall down at once
And say, 'Eat me, my boy.'

Grandma Gurney

Grandma Gurney
Gives to me
Gooseberry tart
And hot sweet tea.

She sits up high
On her rocking chair.
She can't touch the floor
But she doesn't care.

Grandma Gurney
Is tiny and grey.
I wonder if
She'll shrink away?

Grandma Gurney
Has grown very small.
One day she won't be
There at all.

A. E. Dudley

The Ferryman

'Ferry me across the water,
  Do, boatman, do.'
'If you've a penny in your purse
  I'll ferry you.'

'I have a penny in my purse,
  And my eyes are blue;
So ferry me across the water,
  Do, boatman, do.'

'Step into my ferry-boat,
  Be they black or blue,
And for the penny in your purse
  I'll ferry you.'

Christina Rossetti

Where go the Boats?

Dark brown is the river,
Golden is the sand,
It flows along for ever,
With trees on either hand.

Green leaves a-floating,
Castles of the foam.
Boats of mine a-boating –
Where will all come home?

On goes the river,
And out past the mill,
Away down the valley,
Away down the hill.

Away down the river,
A hundred miles or more,
Other little children
Shall bring my boats ashore.

Robert Louis Stevenson

The Voyage

Long long ago, there was a ship
With sails so big and white.
It had ten sailors and Captain Jones,
When it sailed into the night.

It sailed away into the night,
It sailed into the day;
On and on upon the sea
It ploughed its billowing way.

'Oh Captain Jones, where do we go?'
The sailors did demand.
'For fifty days we've voyaged on
And never sighted land.'

'You will never see land again, me lads,'
The captain cried with glee.
'For I have vowed to sail forever
Over the rolling sea.'

'For ever and a day, me lads,
With the wind in our whitened sails,
And up in the sky the wheeling gulls,
And deep in the sea, the whales.

Sometimes the sun will blister your skin.
Sometimes the winds will howl.
Sometimes the snow will freeze your bones
In the seas where icebergs prowl.

But we shall be free, as free as air,
To go where the dolphins play,
So vow with me to sail forever,
Forever and a day.'

The sailors laughed. The sailors cheered.
'Aye, aye, sir, Captain Jones.'
'We'll sail with you till we're old and grey
And the fishes eat our bones.'

So on they sailed 'neath the silvery moon,
Neath the burning sun and the rain,
And of Captain Jones and his sailors ten
We have never heard again.

Joan Prince

Coral

O sailor, come ashore,
  What have you brought for me?
Red coral, white coral,
  Coral from the sea.

I did not dig it from the ground,
  Nor pluck it from the sea;
Feeble insects made it
  In the stormy sea.

Christina Rossetti

The Dandelion

'O Dandelion, yellow as gold,
What do you do all day?'
'I just wait here in the tall green grass
Till the children come to play.'

'O Dandelion, yellow as gold,
What do you do all night?'
'I wait and wait till the cool dews fall,
And my hair grows long and white.'

'And what do you do when your hair is white,
And the children come to play?'
'They take me up in their dimpled hands,
And blow my hair away'.

Here we come a-piping

Here we come a-piping
In springtime and in May;
Green fruit a-ripening,
And winter fled away.
The Queen she sits upon the strand,
Fair as a lily, white as a wand;
Seven billows on the sea,
Horses riding fast and free,
And bells beyond the sand.

Sweet Peas

Here are sweet peas, on tiptoe for a flight;
With wings of gentle flush o'er delicate white,
And taper fingers catching at all things,
To bind them all about with tiny rings.

John Keats

Sing-song

Bread and milk for breakfast,
 And woollen frocks to wear,
And a crumb for robin redbreast
 On the cold days of the year.

Christina Rossetti

Betty and I

Betty my sister and I fell out.
And what do you think it was all about?
She loved coffee and I loved tea,
And that was the reason we could not agree.

There was a Pig

  There was a pig
  Went out to dig
Christmas Day, Christmas Day,
  There was a pig
  Went out to dig
On Christmas Day in the morning.

  There was a sow
  Went out to plough
Christmas Day, Christmas Day,
  There was a sow
  Went out to plough
On Christmas Day in the morning.

  There was a sparrow
  Went out to harrow
Christmas Day, Christmas Day,
  There was a sparrow
  Went out to harrow
On Christmas Day in the morning.

There was a crow
Went out to sow
Christmas Day, Christmas Day,
There was a crow
Went out to sow
On Christmas Day in the morning.

There was a sheep
Went out to reap
Christmas Day, Christmas Day,
There was a sheep
Went out to reap
On Christmas Day in the morning.

Cats sleep anywhere

Cats sleep
Anywhere,
Any table,
Any chair,
Top of piano,
Window ledge,
In the middle,
On the edge,
Open drawer,
Empty shoe,
Anybody's
Lap will do.
Fitted in a
Cardboard box,
In a cupboard
With your frocks –
Anywhere!
They don't care;
Cats sleep
Anywhere.

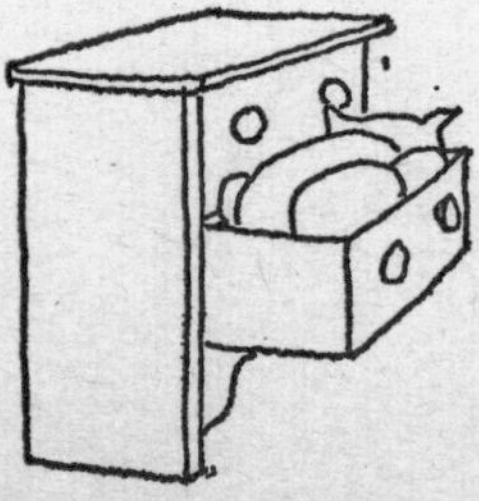

Eleanor Farjeon

Cat in Moonlight

Through moonlight's milk
She slowly passes
As soft as silk
Between tall grasses.
I watch her go
So sleek and white,
As white as snow,
The moon so bright
I hardly know
White moon, white fur,
Which is the light
And which is her.

Douglas Gibson

John Cook's Mare

John Cook had a little grey mare,
  He haw hum!
Her back stood up and her bones were bare.
  He haw hum.

John Cook was riding up Shuter's Bank,
  He haw hum!
And there his nag did kick and prank.
  He haw hum.

John Cook was riding up Shuter's Hill,
  He haw hum!
His mare fell down and she made her will!
  He haw hum.

The bridle and saddle were laid on the shelf.
  He haw hum!
If you want any more, you must make it yourself.
  He haw hum!

Three Warm Pennies

In the morning,
Oh, how grand,
Three warm pennies
In my hand.
Run and skip,
And run and hop,
Until I reach
The little shop.
Click the latch
And push the door
And ding the bell:
Now what's in store?
Mint imperials
In glass jars,
Bubble gum
Or toffee bars?
Liquorice laces,
Fruits and chocs,
Or gobstoppers from
A cardboard box?
Sherbet dip
Or barley stick,

Or sucky fish?
How hard to pick.
In the morning,
Oh, how grand,
Three warm pennies
In my hand.

A. E. Dudley

Song of the Whale

If you ever,
ever,
ever,
ever,
ever,
If you ever, ever, ever see a whale,
You must never,
never,
never,
never,
never,
You must never never tread upon his tail!

If you ever,
ever,
ever,
ever,
ever,
If you ever ever tread upon his tail,

You will never,
never,
never,
never,
never,
You will never live to see another whale!

Skate

Flitting the sea-bed, wide and flat,
I am a fish to wonder at:

a kind-of, sort-of, soft thick square,
like a slow plane in watery air,

with a tough white spine from tail to lips
and straight bones out to my side-wing-tips.

No other interests interest me,
being this is my whole activity.

Alan Brownjohn

Daddy Fell into the Pond

Everyone grumbled. The sky was grey.
We had nothing to do and nothing to say.
We were nearing the end of a dismal day.
And there seemed to be nothing beyond,
  Then
    Daddy fell into the pond!

And everyone's face grew merry and bright,
And Timothy danced for sheer delight.
'Give me the camera, quick, oh quick!
He's crawling out of the duckweed!' Click!

Then the gardener suddenly slapped his knee,
And doubled up, shaking silently,
And the ducks all quacked as if they were daft
And it sounded as if the old drake laughed.
O, there wasn't a thing that didn't respond
  When
    Daddy fell into the pond!

Alfred Noyes

I Saw a Jolly Hunter

I saw a jolly hunter
  With a jolly gun
Walking in the country
  In the jolly sun.

In the jolly meadow
  Sat a jolly hare.
Saw the jolly hunter.
  Took jolly care

Hunter jolly eager –
  Sight of jolly prey.
Forgot gun pointing
  Wrong jolly way.

Jolly hunter jolly head
  Over heels gone.
Jolly old safety-catch
  Not jolly on.

Bang went the jolly gun.
  Hunter jolly dead.
Jolly hare got clean away.
  Jolly good, I said.

Charles Causley

Four Little Girls

Four little girls on a summer day
Went along to the beach to play.
            Sandcastles
            Seashells
            Sea
            And sun,
This is the place for holiday fun.

            But it rained.

Rain, rain, go away:
Four little girls just want to play.
Away went the clouds. The sun came out.
Four little girls began to shout:
            Hooray!

All too soon the day was gone:
Four tired and happy little girls went home.

A. E. Dudley

The Tree on the Hill

There was a tree upon a hill,
The finest tree you ever did see,
And the tree was on the hill,
And the hill stood still,
And the green grass grew around, around, around,
The green grass grew around.

There was a bough upon that tree,
The finest bough you ever did see,
And the bough was on the tree,
And the tree was on the hill,
And the hill stood still,
And the green grass grew around, around, around,
The green grass grew around.

There was a branch upon that bough,
The finest branch you ever did see,
And the branch was on the bough,
And the bough was on the tree,
And the tree was on the hill,
And the hill stood still,
And the green grass grew around, around, around,
The green grass grew around.

There was a twig upon that branch
The finest twig you ever did see,
And the twig was on the branch,
And the branch was on the bough,
And the bough was on the tree,
And the tree was on the hill,
And the hill stood still,
And the green grass grew around, around, around,
The green grass grew around.

There was a leaf upon that twig,
The finest leaf you ever did see,
And the leaf was on the twig,
And the twig was on the branch,
And the branch was on the bough,
And the bough was on the tree,
And the tree was on the hill,
And the hill stood still,
And the green grass grew around, around, around,
The green grass grew around.

There was a nest upon that leaf,
The finest nest you ever did see,

And the nest was on the leaf,
And the leaf was on the twig,
And the twig was on the branch,
And the branch was on the bough,
And the bough was on the tree,
And the tree was on the hill,
And the hill stood still,
And the green grass grew around, around; around,
The green grass grew around.

There was a bird upon that nest,
The finest bird you ever did see,
And the bird was on the nest,
And the nest was on the leaf,
And the leaf was on the twig,
And the twig was on the branch,
And the branch was on the bough,
And the bough was on the tree,
And the tree was on the hill,
And the hill stood still,
And the green grass grew around, around, around;
The green grass grew around.

There was a wing upon that bird,
The finest wing you ever did see,
And the wing was on the bird,
And the bird was on the nest,
And the nest was on the leaf,
And the leaf was on the twig,
And the twig was on the branch,
And the branch was on the bough,
And the bough was on the tree,
And the tree was on the hill,
And the hill stood still,
And the green grass grew around, around, around,
The green grass grew around.

There was a feather upon that wing,
The finest feather you ever did see,
And the feather was on the wing,
And the wing was on the bird,
And the bird was on the nest,
And the nest was on the leaf,
And the leaf was on the twig,
And the twig was on the branch,
And the branch was on the bough,

And the bough was on the tree,
And the tree was on the hill,
And the hill stood still,
And the green grass grew around, around, around,
The green grass grew around.

Jumping Jane

'Jumping Jane, Jumping Jane,
Won't you please
Come out of the rain?
You have no coat on,
Have no hat.
What will mother say to that?'

Jumping Jane leaps on and on.
One more jump and she'll have gone
Round the corner
And up the lane,
And then we may never see her again.

'Jumping high, jumping low,
Twisting, turning as you go,
Jumping Jane, why can't you stop?
Why do you hop,
                    and hop,
                              and hop?'
Jumping Jane said with a smile,
'I must jump on till I've jumped a mile.'

She waved her hand, and gave a grin.
'I'll be back,
As soon as ever I win.'

She went round the corner and up the lane,
And we never,
ever,
saw her again.

Joan Prince

Snow Maidens

Like little fallen drops
of snow
fair maidens
in my garden grow.

Each maid
a small green bodice wears,
and in her ballet gown
appears.

Where chilly winds
blow cool and sweet,
white maidens
in their dancing meet –

And as they move,
how fine to see
their petticoat
embroidery!

Norah Hussey

Hurry Home

You had better hurry home for your supper's nearly ready,
Your mother's in the kitchen and she's awfully wild,
She's been shouting at the cat, and she keeps on saying,
'O where has he got to, the wretched child?'

She has been to the front door and looked through the window,
And now she's banging on the frying pan,
The plates and the dishes are all on the table,
So run, my boy, as fast as you can.

Don't you know that she's cooking your favourite supper,
Potatoes in their jackets and a beefsteak pie?
She's made a jug of custard for the pudding in the oven,
Get a move on, Joe, the stars are in the sky.

They've all left the factory, the streets will soon be empty,
No more playing now, it's time you fed,
It really is a shame to keep your mother waiting,
So come and have your supper, and then off to bed.

Leonard Clark

Finders-keepers

The child said,
'It's an aeroplane, with a tail and wings:
Let me have it;
I'm a pilot,
I can fly to where the sky begins.'

The boy said,
'It's a sword; the blade is whittled fine:
I'm a knight,
I can fight and slay the dragon;
It should be mine.'

The girl said,
'It was I who found it;
It belongs to me:
I'll plant it;
See, the arms are branches;
They will blossom and bear leaves;
It is a tree.'

Cicely Barnes

Explorers

The furry moth explores the night,
  The fish discover cities drowned,
And moles and worms and ants explore
  The many cupboards underground.

The soaring lark explores the sky,
  And gulls explore the stormy seas.
The busy squirrel rummages
  Among the attics of the trees.

James Reeves

My Mother saw a Dancing Bear

My mother saw a dancing bear
By the schoolyard, a day in June.
The keeper stood with chain and bar
And whistle-pipe, and played a tune.

And bruin lifted up its head
And lifted up its dusty feet,
And all the children laughed to see
It caper in the summer heat.

They watched as for the Queen it died.
They watched it march. They watched it halt.
They heard the keeper as he cried,
'Now, roly-poly!' 'Somersault!'

And then, my mother said, there came
The keeper with a begging-cup,
The bear with burning coat of fur
Shaming the laughter to a stop.

They paid a penny for the dance,
But what they saw was not the show;
Only, in bruin's aching eyes,
Far-distant forests, and the snow.

Charles Causley

Fireworks

They rise like sudden fiery flowers
That burst upon the night,
Then fall to earth in burning showers
Of crimson, blue and white.

Like buds too wonderful to name,
Each miracle unfolds,
And catherine-wheels begin to flame
Like whirling marigolds.

Rockets and roman-candles make
An orchard of the sky,
When magic trees their petals shake
Upon each gazing eye.

James Reeves

The Little Toy Land of the Dutch

Away, 'way off 'cross the seas and such
Lies the little flat land of the Dutch, Dutch, Dutch!

Where the green toy meadows stretch off to the sea,
With a little canal where a fence ought to be!

Where the windmills' arms go round, round, round,
And sing to the cows with a creaky sound.

Where storks live up in the chimney top,
And wooden shoes sound plop, plop, plop!

Where little toy houses stand in a row,
And dog carts clattering past them go.

Where milk cans shine in the shiniest way,
And the housemaids scrub, scrub, scrub all day.

Where dikes keep out the raging sea,
And shut in the land as snug as can be.

Oh, that little toy land, I like it so much,
That prim little, trim little, land of the Dutch!

This Old Man

This old man
He played One,
He played nick-nack on my drum.
Nick-nack, paddy whack,
Give a dog a bone,
This old man came rolling home.

This old man
He played Two,
He played nick-nack on my shoe.
Nick-nack, paddy whack,
Give a dog a bone,
This old man came rolling home.

This old man
He played Three,
He played nick-nack on my knee.
Nick-nack, paddy whack,
Give a dog a bone,
This old man came rolling home.

This old man
He played Four,
He played nick-nack on my door.
Nick-nack, paddy whack,
Give a dog a bone,
This old man came rolling home.

This old man
He played Five,
He played nick-nack on my hive.
Nick-nack, paddy whack,
Give a dog a bone,
This old man came rolling home.

This old man
He played Six,
He played nick-nack on my sticks.
Nick-nack, paddy whack,
Give a dog a bone,
This old man came rolling home.

This old man,
He played Seven,
He played nick-nack down to Devon.
Nick-nack, paddy whack,
Give a dog a bone,
This old man came rolling home.

This old man
He played Eight,
He played nick-nack on my gate.
Nick-nack, paddy whack,
Give a dog a bone,
This old man came rolling home.

This old man
He played Nine,
He played nick-nack on my line.
Nick-nack, paddy whack,
Give a dog a bone,
This old man came rolling home.

This old man
He played Ten,
He played nick-nack on my hen.
Nick-nack, paddy whack,
Give a dog a bone,
This old man came rolling home.

Rabbit and Lark

'Under the ground
  It's rumbly and dark
And interesting,'
  Said Rabbit to Lark.

Said Lark to Rabbit,
  'Up in the sky
There's plenty of room
  And it's airy and high.'

'Under the ground
  It's warm and dry.
Won't you live with me?'
  Was Rabbit's reply.

'The air's so sunny.
  I wish you'd agree,'
Said the little Lark,
  'To live with me.'

But under the ground
  And up in the sky,
Larks can't burrow
  Nor rabbits fly.

So Skylark over
  And Rabbit under
They had to settle
  To live asunder.

And often these two friends
  Meet with a will
For a chat together
  On top of the hill.

James Reeves

The Piffle-poffle

If you ever see a creature
With thirty-seven toes
And eyes of an enormous size
And a nose which Grows and Grows,
Be on your best behaviour
And treat him with Great Care,
(Which means refrain from laughing
At the colour of his hair)
And he might take you home with him
To have tea in his lair.
In which case, do not mention
The fact that he is green,
Nor that he is slightly plump
(He likes to think he's lean)
Pretend you haven't noticed
His thirty-seven toes,
And say 'How most convenient
To have a nose which grows!'
But never, ever tell him
That his mouth is rather wide
Or you might get a close look at
His reddish-black inside!

If you do not ask him why
He eats without a knife
Then in the Piffle-poffle
You have a friend for life!

Catherine Lodge (aged 12)

Look at all those Monkeys

Look at all those monkeys
Jumping in their cage;
Why don't they all go out to work
And earn a decent wage?

How can you say such silly things,
And you a son of mine?
Imagine monkeys travelling on
The Morden-Edgware line!

But what about the pekinese!
They have an allocation.
'Don't travel during Peke hour'
It says on every station.

My Gosh, you're right, my clever boy,
I never thought of that!
And so they left the monkey house,
While an elephant raised his hat.

Spike Milligan

I took my Wife to Market

I took my wife to market
  It was not market day.
We had a hundred hens' eggs
  That never a fowl did lay.

We rode there in a trap, sir,
  Had neither wheel nor brake,
And from the yellow stable
  The pony did not take.

When we got to the market
  It was the crack of noon,
High in the tower the hooting owl
  And in the sky the moon.

And when we sold the eggs, sir,
  For neither coin nor gear,
We went into an ale-house
  That sold not wine nor beer.

We sat down by the church-yard
  When to eat we were fain.
The cheese it was not made of milk,
  Nor the bread from grain.

And when the fair was over
  We made our homeward way,
Deep in the west the dying moon
  And in the east the day.

I opened up my door, sir,
  No latch nor key had I,
And as we went downstairs to bed
  I heard the cockerel cry.

Although for years a thousand
  Upon this earth I be,
I want not such a day again
  For all the Queen's fee.

And though for years a thousand
  On earth I may grow old
I want not such a day again
  For all the King's gold.

Charles Causley

Soft Landings

Space-man, space-man,
Blasting off the ground
With a wake of flame behind you,
Swifter than passing sound.

Space-man, ace-man,
Shooting through the air,
Twice around the moon and back
Simply because it's there.

Space-man, place-man,
Cruising through the skies
To plant your flags on landscapes
Unknown to human eyes.

Space-man – Race, man,
Scorching back to earth –
To home and friends and everything
That gives your mission worth.

Howard Sergeant

I Had a Little Space Man

I had a little space man
and nothing would he wear
but a deadly ray tube
and blue, straggly hair.

The Duke of Loam's daughter
wouldn't come to stay
and all on account of
that little deadly ray.

Michael Ivens

Index of Authors

Index of First Lines